IT'S A
FUNGUS
AMONG
US

CARLA BILLUPS & DAWN CUSICK

IT'S A
FUNGUS
AMONG
US

THE GOOD, THE BAD
& THE DOWNRIGHT
SCARY

CARLA BILLUPS & DAWN CUSICK

MoonDance

Quarto is the authority on a wide range of topics.
Quarto educates, entertains, and enriches the lives of our readers—
enthusiasts and lovers of hands-on living.
www.quartoknows.com

MoonDance

6 Orchard Road, Suite 100
Lake Forest, CA 92630
quartoknows.com
Visit our blogs at quartoknows.com

Printed in China
1 3 5 7 9 10 8 6 4 2

MIX
Paper from
responsible sources
FSC® C101537

CONTENTS

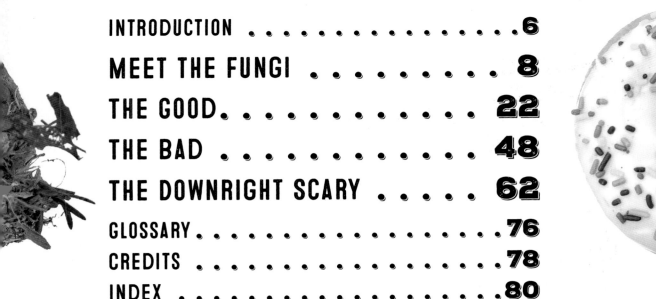

INTRODUCTION

Sometimes, people can't seem to help themselves. We want to label things just one way. Are fungi good? Are fungi bad? Or are they downright scary? Which is it? To answer these questions, you probably need to learn a lot more about fungi.

When you picture a fungus, you may have a mushroom in mind. As you will see, there's a lot more to fungi than mushrooms. Fungi spores are super small, while the largest part of a fungus often lives underground. Some underground fungi are so large you can see them from space!

Fungi live all over the world, even in outer space, where they can hitchhike on spaceships. Many fungi like dark, warm, damp habitats, but others live in the Arctic and in deserts. Some even live on and in plants and animals. More than eighty kinds of fungi live just in the fur of three-toed sloths.

Mushrooms and other fruiting bodies don't usually live long, but the fungi they are attached to can live for hundreds or even thousands of years. Fruiting bodies come in some wild colors and shapes — some even glow in the dark!

Fungi are very important to food webs. Many animals eat fungi, from the smallest bacteria to nematodes and mites to squirrels and monkeys. Some animals eat nothing but

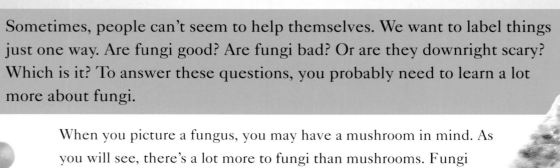

fungi! Even more important, fungi break down feces and dead plants and animals, making nutrients available to other plants and animals. Fungi are important to people, too. We can thank fungi for bread, donuts, sour candy, stretchy pizza cheese, and some vitamins and medicines.

Fungi also clean the environment in many ways. They pull toxins from the air, decompose feces and dead plants and animals, and break down plastic trash and radiation. Fungi add nutrients to the soil and make the ground strong enough for baseball fields and skating rinks. They also help plants talk to each other and help people solve crimes. What's not to like about fungi?

After all the good things that fungi do, why would anyone argue that fungi are bad or downright scary? Well, if your feet are itching from athlete's foot, you may believe fungi are bad, bad, bad. Moldy messes, plant parasites, and decomposing bodies may end your debate.

Some fungi may cause some frogs, salamanders, snakes, bats, corals, and plants to go extinct. Other fungi change animals into zombies, making them look and behave in weird ways. Still other fungi can wipe out crops that feed billions of people around the world.

So, what do you think? Good? Bad? Downright scary? All three? One thing's for sure: fungi are absolutely amazing. After you have finished this book, do the world's fungi a favor: share some of what you've learned with people who think fungi are nothing more than mushrooms.

Carla Billups

Dawn Cusick

LANGUAGE MATTERS

The Greek word for fungi is *myco*, and people who study fungi are called mycologists. You may be wondering about the difference between *fungus* and *fungi*. The first word describes just one fungus. The plural form of the word *fungus* is *fungi*. The adjective form of *fungi* is *fungal*.

YOU MAY BE WONDERING . . .

What, exactly, is a fungus? A fungus is a eukaryote that absorbs its food. (In case you've forgotten, a eukaryote is a complex cell with a nucleus.) There are other types of eukaryotes, but they get their food in different ways. Plants make their own food through photosynthesis, while animals ingest their food.

A NUMBERS GAME

More than 130,000 types of fungi have been named as species. There may be more than a million and a half undiscovered species. Yowza, that's a lot of fungi!

HELLO, COUSIN!

Many years ago, fungi were grouped with plants. This grouping made sense at the time. Both fungi and plants have cell walls. They both have root-like structures and seem to grow upward. By the 1960s, biologists knew enough about the differences between fungi and plants to place them in separate kingdoms. Then, fungi were considered more primitive than plants.

When biologists began comparing DNA sequences between members of different kingdoms, they found that fungi share more base pairs with animals than they do with plants. Fungi and animals share so many base pairs that fungi were moved closer to animals on family trees.

ENERGY SAVERS

Absorbing your food may seem like a silly way to eat, but when you compare fungi to animals, you may be impressed. When fungi sense nearby food, they grow toward it and use their extra body size to absorb the food. If there's no food nearby, fungi do not waste energy building or maintaining larger bodies. When animals sense nearby food, they can spend a lot of energy finding or chasing it. Whether they find lots of food or none, they must spend a great deal of energy maintaining their digestive systems.

COMPARE & CONTRAST

Check out the ways fungi and animals get food energy from a cheeseburger or a salad. Both fungi and animals use enzymes to break these foods into sugars, lipids, and proteins, but their similarities end there.

Fungi release digestive enzymes outside their bodies. Once the food is broken down, fungi absorb only the nutrients they can use. Fungi spend no energy breaking down or getting rid of waste because it never enters their bodies.

Animals release digestive enzymes inside their bodies. Once the food is broken down, animal bodies still need to deal with waste, which takes a lot of energy. Waste can also carry disease, and many predators use it to find prey. This zebra needs more than one hundred feet (30.5 m) of alimentary canal to digest food and it can only eat plants. Carnivores such as the dog may have shorter alimentary canals, but they can't eat most of the things fungi can eat. How much energy do fungi waste on alimentary canals? *None.*

9

SIZES AND SHAPES

When you think of a fungus, you may have a pizza mushroom in mind. Many fungi come in cool colors and shapes, though. Others are so small that people never see them. Turn the page to learn more!

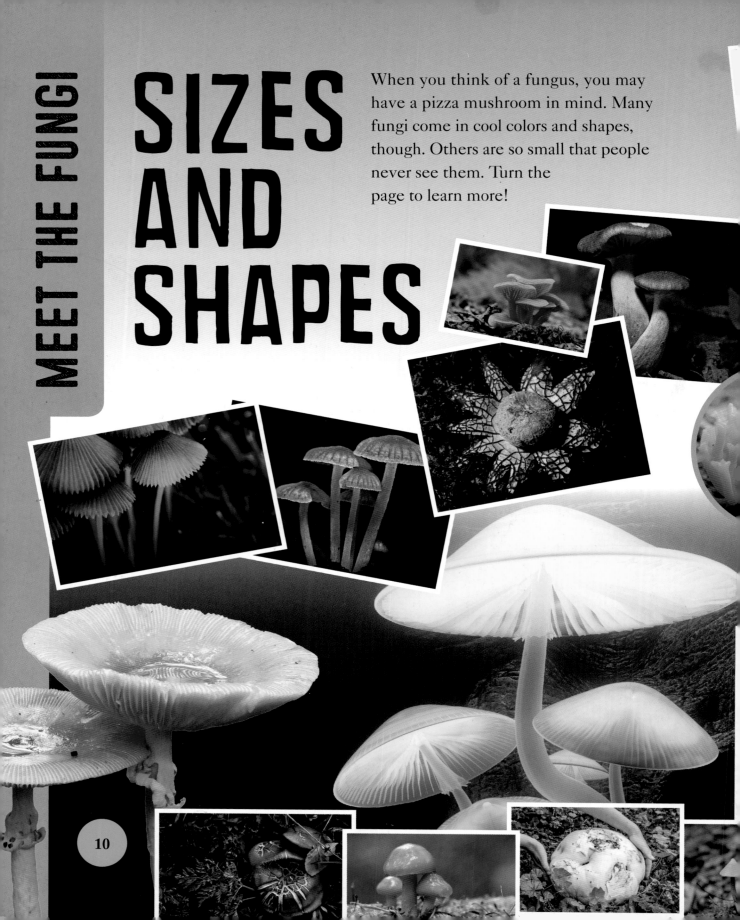

10

ANATOMY

As you will see, there's a lot more to fungi than mushrooms, and not all types of fungi have mushrooms.

IN THE SMALL PICTURE

Some fungi, such as the yeasts, are unicellular. Others are multicellular and a single organism can contain trillions of cells. Each berry-like shape in the photo above is a yeast.

Unlike animal cells, fungi cells are protected by a cell wall made from a complex sugar called chitin (kite-in). Chitin is also found in the exoskeletons of arthropods such as insects, spiders, and crabs. (Plants have cell walls, too, but their cell walls are made from a different complex sugar, cellulose.)

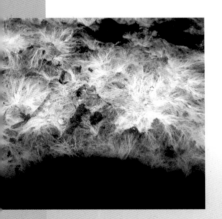

IN THE BIG PICTURE

Humans rarely see most fungi because they are too small or living underground. Root-like threads called hyphae (hi-fee) grow in colonies called mycelia (my-sell-ee-ah). These colonies contain many thin threads that can look fuzzy or hairy. Don't believe it? Check out the edges of a fungus on a Petri dish . . . or on the strawberries you left out on the counter yesterday. Fungi release digestive enzymes through these threads.

MUSHROOM ANATOMY

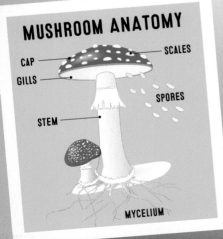

CAP
GILLS
SCALES
SPORES
STEM
MYCELIUM

FRUITING BODIES

Fruiting bodies such as the examples on pages 10 and 11 are signs that fungi live below. When it's time to reproduce, fruiting bodies grow up from mycelia. Some fruiting bodies have gills on the undersides of their caps.

REPRODUCTION

Given how many types of fungi there are, you probably won't be surprised to learn that fungi reproduce in different ways. Some fungi reproduce sexually, producing offspring that genetically are very different from one another. Other fungi make genetic clones of themselves through asexual reproduction. Some fungi shift back and forth, depending on the environment.

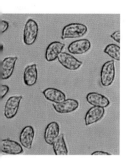

SPORES

Think of spores as seeds, but smaller in size and lighter in weight. When a single fungus reproduces, those spores will be genetic clones. Spores can also be formed through sexual reproduction, and these spores are called zygospores.

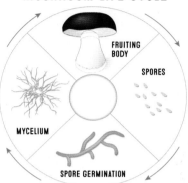

MUSHROOM LIFE CYCLE

FRUITING BODY

SPORES

SPORE GERMINATION

MYCELIUM

SPORES GALORE

A single fruiting body can release trillions of spores at one time. If a spore lands in a good habitat, it grows into a new fungus. The photo below shows spores leaving a puffball in a high-pressure burst. In mushrooms, spores are released through the gills. Spores can also grow along hyphae underground. Some spores move to new places on water or animals. Others move through wind currents. Spores from Asian desert fungi have been found in southern North America, while others have been found high in the atmosphere, above the jet stream.

SPEEDY SPORES

What's the fastest organism on Earth? No, it's not a cheetah. It's a fungus! Scientists clocked a dung-loving spore at twenty-five meters per second with a high-speed camera. These spores go from zero to twenty miles per hour in two millionths of a second. How do they move so fast? Fluids build up under the spores, creating pressure. When the pressure gets too high, the fluid shoots out, taking spores along for the ride.

YEASTS & LICHENS

About 20 percent of fungi species are yeast or lichens (like-enz). Many people don't know much about them, but they affect the world in wild, scary, and wonderful ways.

HELLO, YEAST!

Yeasts are small, single-celled fungi. They live around the world, in water and on land. Many species live on and inside animals, too. Yeasts are not as fun to look at or as easy to find as many other kinds of fungi.

LIKING LICHENS

Some lichens are a partnership between fungi and algae or cyanobacteria. Other lichens are three-way partnerships between fungi, algae, and cyanobacteria. Lichens can live through long droughts, and some can live for hundreds of years.

A GOOD DEAL

A lichen symbiosis is called a mutualism because both (or all three!) organisms benefit from their partnership. The fungi in lichens do not need soil. They can attach to surfaces such as rocks and trees that algae and cyanobacteria cannot.

Fungi also provide the moisture that algae and cyanobacteria need. Lichen fungi can absorb water from rain, fog, and even humidity in the air. Algae and cyanobacteria make food energy with photosynthesis. Fungi get vitamins, sugars, and proteins from their photosynthesizing partners.

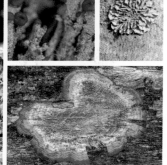

COLORS & SHAPES

Not all lichens look like thin, green circles. Some have cup or spike shapes, while others look like small bushes. Many come in bright colors.

CHECK IT OUT

Collect a broken stem or branch with lichens on it. Look at the lichen with a dissecting microscope or a strong magnifying glass. Scrape away a layer of the lichen and look again. The fungus part of the lichen will look like lots of threads. You may see some green areas, too, from chlorophyll in algae or cyanobacteria cells where photosynthesis happens.

TEST IT OUT

YOU MAY HAVE HEARD THAT LICHENS ONLY GROW ON THE NORTH SIDES OF TREES AND THAT YOU CAN USE THEM LIKE A COMPASS IF YOU GET LOST IN THE WOODS. IS THIS TRUE WHERE YOU LIVE?

WHAT YOU NEED

Notebook
Pencil
Handheld compass or compass app
Calculator
Trees

WHAT TO DO

1. Find some trees with lichens. Use your compass to find out which direction on the trees the lichens grow. Write down the direction for each tree in your notebook. Write down the degrees, too, if your compass gives them to you.

2. As you start collecting data, think about other questions you can research while you're outside. Do lichens grow nearer the bottoms or tops of trees? Do they grow on one type of tree more than on another? Or on larger trees more than on smaller trees?

3. After you go back inside, look at your data sheet. Think about ways you can describe your data with numbers and pictures. If you recorded directions such as north and northwest, can you figure out how often you saw each direction in percentages? If you recorded your data in degrees, can you figure out the mean and standard deviations? Now that you have data, what do you think? Would it be a good idea to use lichens to find your way home?

15

HABITATS

Fungi live all over the world. Many fungi live in dark, damp places, while others live in harsh habitats. Sometimes fungi live on their own, but many live with other organisms in partnerships or as parasites.

LIVING NEAR FOOD

Fungi that feed on feces or dead plants and animals often live in shady, wooded areas.

HOT SPOTS

You've probably heard that the water in hot springs and geysers in Yellowstone National Park is very hot. Did you know that the soil around these waters is also hot? Hot springs panic grass can live in Yellowstone soils up to 145 degrees F (63° C) because a fungus living on grass's roots protects them.

HOME, SWEET HOME

Many fungi make their homes on other organisms such as plants and animals. Not impressed? The three-toed sloth's fur is full of fungus. Eighty-four types of fungi from the sloth's fur have been collected and studied. These fungi may be helping the sloths fight disease. There's still a lot of research to be done.

SALT LOVERS

Although most land fungi cannot live in salty places, a few types thrive in salty places.

COOL DUDES

Biologists have found a fungus living under and between rocks in Antarctica. *Brrrrr.*

WATER!

Fungi live in oceans, rivers, streams, lakes, ponds, and even puddles.

17

LICHEN HABITATS

Because lichens can live for years without much food or water, they can live in places that many plants cannot. In some habitats, lichens are the main producers in the food chain. You can also find them in forests and on neighborhood trees.

FIRE LICHENS?

The Bay of Fires is found on the east coast of the Australian island Tasmania. The granite rocks that line its beach are covered with bright-red lichens. The Bay of Fires was named in the 1700s by a boat captain who saw glowing fires built by Aborigines.

DESERT LICHENS

Lichens live in deserts and harsh habitats all over the world, from the Namib Desert in South Africa to the Lapland mountain tundra in Finland, to Yellowstone National Park in the US.

ARCTIC LICHENS

The fall colors of Arctic lichens may look pretty to humans, but for wild animals that live there, lichens are an important food source. In the winter, many animals dig under the snow to find lichens.

FAKE FUNGUS

Just because something looks like a fungus or is named after one, doesn't make it one. Remember: if it's a fungus, it needs to be a member of the kingdom Fungi.

YOU BELONG IN MOVIES!

Top right: Hike through the Karkonosze Mountains in Poland and you may come across this mushroom-shaped rock. There are more rocks like this one in nearby mountains. Glaciers helped form these rocks.

Below and right: Near the middle of Turkey you can find mushroom-shaped rocks in many shapes and sizes. They were formed by natural erosion over many, many years.

FUNGUS OR ANIMAL?

Lacewing insects do not look like fungi, but their eggs sure do! In fact, for a long time, people thought the eggs were a fungus. Biologists are not sure why lacewings lay their eggs this way. It may be to confuse predators, or it may be to keep newly hatched lacewings from eating each other!

YOU'VE BEEN SLIMED!

When there's not enough food, slime molds do something wild. They merge their bodies together into one giant cell that moves through the world the way amoebae do, by contracting and expanding. Slime molds come in many colors and shapes.

MAZE GAMES

Curious about how slime molds form, biologists did some experiments with mazes. They chopped up a large slime mold and placed the pieces in different places in the maze. In just a few hours, the pieces had grown and reconnected with one another in the maze. Without brains or sense organs such as eyes, how did the pieces find one another?

Biologists did other experiments in mazes, too. When they placed food in the mazes, the slime molds took the shortest routes through the mazes to get to the food. They also went to the foods that had the most nutrition in them. *Wow*.

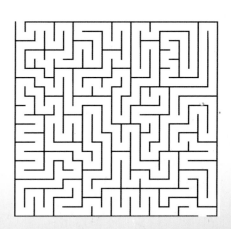

WEATHER

Can fungi affect weather, and maybe even climate? Mushroom spores may hold part of the answer. Each year mushrooms release more than fifty million tons of spores. These spores travel through the air and land in other places to grow.

HIGH IN THE SKY

Clouds don't just form out of thin air. Instead, water droplets need something small to attach to. This process is called cloud seeding. Dust, pollution, pollen, and even mushroom spores can seed clouds!

RAIN DROPS

Some spores travel high into the atmosphere. When the air is humid, small water droplets attach to spores because a type of sugar in them attracts water. As more and more water droplets collect on the spores, clouds begin to form. When droplets in the clouds get heavy enough, they fall down as rain.

A GOOD DEAL

Mushrooms need damp habitats. When mushroom spores seed clouds, they help provide the rain and damp habitats in which they need to live.

OVER THE AMAZON

Organic particles in the air collect water droplets. These carbon particles are so small they must join with other carbon particles to be big enough to collect water droplets. Potassium salts help join them together. In the Amazon rain forest, some of this potassium comes from fungus! When mushrooms shoot out their spores, they also shoot out potassium. High in the sky, the potassium salts stick to the carbon particles, which can seed clouds and cause rain.

MAKING WIND

To get the spores into the air, scientists have found some mushrooms create their own weather. Before releasing their spores, mushrooms release water vapor. This water vapor cools the air around the mushroom. The cooler air sinks and the warmer air around the mushroom rises, creating small convection currents. These currents cause small winds that lift the spores up about four inches (10 cm), where they may be carried away by larger winds.

FIELD TRIP

Go into the woods at night with a flashlight. If there are certain kinds of mushrooms in the area, you may see spores releasing into the air.

23

FORENSIC FUNGUS

Police and crime investigators can use fungus to solve crimes. This type of crime solving is called forensic mycology.

FUNGAL FINGERPRINTS

As people move around, they pick up traces of fungus. The fungus acts like a fingerprint, connecting people to the places they have been. Investigators can find fungal spores on plants, soil, human bodies, concrete, brick, plastic, and many other things.

TIME & PLACE?

Investigators use forensic mycology to connect victims and suspects. It can help them figure out where a crime happened or a victim's time of death. Fungus can also tell investigators if a body has been moved.

Forensic mycologists can also look at the growth rate of fungus found on dead bodies, which can help them figure out when the victim died. Some types of fungi grow only on dead bodies, while others only grow on living bodies.

GET A JOB!

There are not many forensic mycologists now because the field is so new. The evidence they discover can only be used in court if they know a lot about fungi and work hard not to make mistakes during their investigations.

TROUBLE WITH TRUFFLES

Truffles are considered the most expensive food in the world. These fungi grow underground, near certain types of trees. People use pigs and specially trained dogs to sniff them out.

When lots of money is involved, there is crime. There are many cases of fungi fraud. Low-quality truffles are passed off for higher-quality truffles. Some restaurants are robbed of their truffles, and truffle hunters have been robbed on their own property. Truffle-sniffing dogs have been stolen, too. Local and international police have investigated these crimes.

WOW, PLANTS!

You may think you know a lot about the way plants live. Boy, oh boy, are you in for some surprises. There's so much more to plants than leaves, seeds, and flowers.

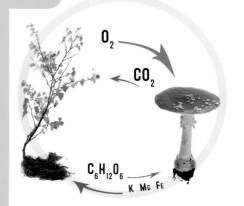

O_2

CO_2

$C_6H_{12}O_6$

K Mg Fe

PLANT PARTNERS

Most land plants live with fungi in a symbiosis called mycorrhizae (my-ko-ry-zee). Underground, plant roots connect with the root-like threads of fungi colonies. The plants get water, phosphorus, and nitrogen from the fungi with which they live. The fungi get sugars from the plants.

HEALTHIER WITH FUNGUS?

When plant roots live with fungi, their immune systems work better, which helps them fight disease. Plants living with fungi also grow faster and grow larger. See the glowing red areas in the photo to the left? Those are places where a fungus is helping plant roots release chemicals. These chemicals help plants by changing the soil's pH and removing toxins.

HERE I AM!

How do fungi find plant roots? Plants secrete chemicals in their roots that attract fungi and helpful bacteria.

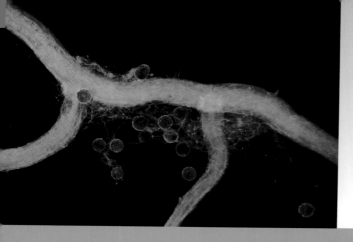

INSIDE? OUTSIDE?

Some mycorrhizae live in between cells on the inside of roots and grow out into the soil around them. Others live outside of roots. In this photo, you can see the mycorrhizae on the outside of a corn plant's roots. The round circles are spores.

VIEW FROM ABOVE

Believe it or not, you can see underground fungi from space! In this overhead photo of a forest from a space satellite, the brown areas are tree roots and the white and yellow areas are fungi.

TEST IT OUT

YOU CAN DO SOME PLANT EXPERIMENTS TO MEASURE HOW MUCH FUNGI CAN HELP A PLANT.

WHAT YOU NEED

Plant seedlings, at least two about the same size (more is better!)

Mycorrhizae (look for it in stores that sell plants)

Craft paintbrush

WHAT TO DO

1. Divide your plants into two groups.
2. Following the instructions on the label, paint the mycorrhizae onto the roots of the plants in one group. Do not add mycorrhizae to the plants in the other group. Label the two groups so you will know which plant(s) received which treatment.
3. Allow the plants to grow. Be sure they get the same amount of sunlight and the same amount of water.
4. Measure the plant(s) in each group and compare them. You can measure them by weight, height, length of roots, size of leaves, or number of leaves or buds.

WORLD-WIDE WEB

New science research shows that some plants share information and food with one another through mycelia threads that may connect even faraway plants the way the Internet connects computers on the web.

CHATTY PLANTS

Plants share information about predators such as aphids with their neighbors through mycelia. In experiments with bean plants, biologists found that when aphids started eating one plant, its neighbors started releasing chemicals to help them fight aphids. How did neighboring plants learn that aphids were nearby? The information moved from the roots of one plant to the roots of others through mycelia.

In other experiments with tomato plants, biologists found the plants warned their neighbors about a disease-causing fungus through mycelia. *Wild!*

STOP, THIEF!

Some plants take carbon from neighbors through mycelia. Other plants feed on fungi instead of making their own food with photosynthesis. Examples of parasite plants include some orchid and heath plants.

SUPER SHARERS

Biologists were surprised to learn that some plants share carbon and other nutrients with neighboring plants. These nutrients move from one plant to another through mycelia. For young plants, these extra nutrients can help them survive.

BACK OFF!

Some plants move chemicals through their roots to mycelia that connect to nearby plant roots. These chemicals may hurt their neighbors.

TERRA FIRMA

How often do you think about what's under the ground you walk, drive, and play on? What makes the ground below you solid? From the ground up and the ground down, fungi change the world.

THE GROUND BENEATH US

In many places, billions of root-like fungi hairs make the ground under us firm. Experiments showed that these hyphae colonies can support more than thirty thousand times their weight. *How* is that possible? Even though single hyphae hairs can be thin, there is strength in numbers. Also, the chitin in their cell walls adds to their strength.

30

SOIL SAVERS

Mycelia also help to hold ground soil in place during heavy rains. How? Fungi release a protein that works like glue, holding small pieces of soil together and keeping them from washing away. This fungal glue also helps soil hold more water.

THE SOIL FOOD WEB

Fungi, bacteria, nematodes, earthworms, protists, and arthropods are important parts of soil food webs. *What?* You've never heard of the soil food web? Fungi make carbon and other nutrients available because they can break down foods that other organisms cannot. Cellulose from plant cell walls, chitin from arthropod exoskeletons, and lignin from older plants are examples of fungi foods that help make soil food webs healthy. Without decomposers such as fungi, there would be no soil!

FUNGUS FEEDERS

From turtles to lemurs, many wild animals eat fungi to get protein, vitamins, and water. Some animals eat fungi as part of their diets, while others eat only fungi. Animals that eat only fungi are called fungivores.

WINTER FOODS

You probably know that many squirrels gather nuts in the fall to save for winter food. Some squirrels also collect mushrooms for winter food. Instead of burying the mushrooms, they hang them in trees. They eat mushrooms during other times of the year, too.

BIRD FOOD?

A few birds eat fungi. Other birds feed on insects and seeds on and near fungi.

32

MUSHROOM MUNCHERS

Some insects, spiders, and millipedes eat fungi, too!

PRIMATE POWER

Many lemurs, gorillas, monkeys, and some other primates eat mushrooms as part of their diets.

SNAIL FOOD

Snails use their teeth to scrape off pieces of mushrooms to eat. Their teeth are made from chitin, the same material as fungi cell walls.

33

FUNGUS FEEDERS

From small invertebrates to large mammals, fungi foods are an important part of everyday life for many animals.

ENDANGERED FUNGI FEEDERS

Golden snub-nosed monkeys feed mostly on lichens. These monkeys are endangered and live in one small area in southwest China. One kind of endangered flying squirrel in North America eats only fungi. The endangered Eurasian red squirrel from Europe and Asia eats lichens.

One endangered reptile, a type of tuatara, doesn't eat fungus. Instead, it uses a glow-in-the-dark fungus growing on its tongue to attract flying insects in dark New Zealand caves.

NAMED FOR FUNGI

Some beetles and gnats feed on fungi. Toxins in the fungus may also help protect them from predators. These insects help the fungi by spreading spores. Left: the pleasing fungus beetle. Right: fungus gnat larvae feeding on fungus

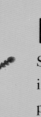

34

FULL HOUSE

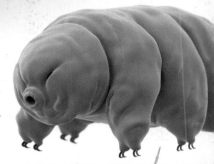

Lichens can be home to thousands of small animals such as water bears, mites, nematodes, and more. Some animals live in lichens for protection from predators, while others live there to feed on algae or cyanobacteria, or to get water. Small predators live in or near lichens to find prey.

CHECK IT OUT

Collect some small pieces of lichens and soak them in distilled water for a few hours. Use a magnifying glass or microscope to find small animals in the water. It may take a while to get used to searching for such small animals, so do not give up too fast.

FUNGUS FARMERS

Deep in the tropical rain forests of South and Central America, leafcutter ants carry pieces of leaves to their underground nests. They don't eat the leaves. Instead, they feed the leaves to a fungus.

Why would nests with up to eight million ants spend energy growing fungus? The ants and the fungus live together in a type of symbiotic relationship called a mutualism. The ants provide a habitat and care for the fungus. They also release some chemicals that work like fertilizer to help the fungus grow. Not impressed yet? The ants also release enzymes from their saliva and bacteria from their feces to help their fungus break down the leaves. The fungus grows high-energy food packages for the ants.

Scientists want to learn more about ant/fungus relationships to help them make biofuels. Right now, only corncobs are used to make biofuels. The stalks and leaves are hard to break down, which makes the process expensive. If scientists can use genes from the fungus to make chemicals that can break down plants, they may be able to make biofuels much faster and for less money. Scientists are also studying bacteria that live with fungus-farming ants in case the bacteria's chemicals can help make biofuels, too.

HIDING *with* LICHENS

Many animals camouflage with lichens to hide from predators. Some predators camouflage with lichens, too. Did you find the hiding animals below right away or did you need to study the photos for a while?

AMBUSH PREDATORS

Lichen huntsman spiders (above) from Australia catch prey on and near lichens. The patterns and colors on their exo-skeletons look like lichens.

CHAMELEON FROGS

In many parts of the world, gray tree frogs camouflage well with lichens. These frogs earned their chameleon-frog nickname because the color cells in their skin can get bigger or smaller when the light or temperature changes.

DON'T MOVE!

Some lizards camouflage well with lichens, too. Like the other animals here, the lizards need to stay very still to blend in well. This short-horned lizard feeds on insects and spiders.

LICHEN-COVERED LACEWINGS

As larvae, some lacewing insects (top left) cover their backs with small pieces of lichens. The lichens help lacewings sneak up on prey such as the aphids. They have large jaws, and they eat so many aphids that they have been nicknamed aphid lions! Adult lacewings (top right) do not wear lichens on their backs.

MORE CAMO!

Other animals that camouflage with lichens include some geckos, beetles, caterpillars, grasshoppers, and katydids.

BUILDING *with* LICHENS

Many animals hide from predators by camouflaging their bodies to lichens. The lichens may also make nests warmer, drier, and may even fight off some bacteria.

BIRD NESTS

Birds press lichen pieces into their nests, helping the nests blend in better in trees and bushes.

HIBERNATION HOMES

Arctic ground squirrels sleep through the long winter in burrows lined with lichens, fur, and leaves.

CROWDED CONDITIONS

Bagworm caterpillars (above left) make bag-like homes in trees by spinning silk around tree stems and adding pieces of plants and lichen to the silk. Adult females lay up to one thousand eggs in a bag!

37

CLEANUP CREW

When you take a walk in the woods or stare up into the sky, the world can look so perfect. Without fungi, the world would look very different. Give fungi some credit!

FECES-FREE

Think about how many animals live in your neighborhood or near your school. From the largest mammals to the smallest spiders, every animal is pooping every day. Wild animals don't have bathrooms and toilets, so why don't we see poop everywhere?

Fungi and bacteria feed on animal feces, and they do it very quickly. In the photos here, you can see two kinds of fungi. On the left, a fungus is feeding on poop from the top down. On the right, the fungus is feeding from the bottom up. The mushrooms will release spores that may land on other piles of poop.

AIR CLEANERS

Some lichens bring pollution-causing dust and other chemicals into their cells. They also help pull carbon dioxide from the air. (Their algae or bacteria partners use CO_2 when they make sugars with photosynthesis.)

Not all lichens can live in polluted habitats. Some lichens cannot live in air polluted with too much sulfur dioxide. Most of the sulfur dioxide in Earth's air comes from humans making electricity from coal and burning gasoline in cars and trucks.

CLEANUP CREW

Does a trash dump or an oil spill look like pollution to you? To some fungi, pollution isn't a problem that needs solving. Instead, it's food energy!

TOXIC CLEANUP

In 1986 in the Ukraine, near Russia, the Chernobyl nuclear plant exploded. Dangerous radiation leaked into the environment, and Chernobyl City was evacuated.

Recently, scientists who study the nuclear site sent robots into the power plant to explore areas that are still highly radioactive. The robots returned with black mold collected from the walls of the nuclear reactor.

Radiation damages the DNA of most organisms, yet this fungus seemed to be thriving around large amounts of radiation. Not only does this fungus grow *toward* radiation instead of away from it, but it also releases more spores when it's near radiation.

Scientists believed the radiation might be helping the mold grow. They were right! Instead of absorbing its food, this type of mold uses a protein called melanin to make its own food from radioactive energy. (Melanin is the same pigment that gives color to your hair and skin.)

OIL SPILLS

Some fungi can help clean up oil spills from water and soil. They feed on oil by breaking it down into sugars.

PLASTIC EATERS

Think about a fungus that could help take on a major pollution problem: plastic. Many types of plastics do not break down naturally. They stay in landfills and in oceans for hundreds of years.

College students found a fungus in the Amazon rain forest that eats polyurethane. Back in the lab, biologists found the enzyme the fungus uses to break down plastic. This discovery may help humans deal with plastic pollution.

HIGH-TECH FUNGI

If you care about the environment, you may try to protect it by recycling household trash or using less electricity. Fungi may change your ideas about ways to go green.

MUSHROOM BATTERIES

One day, maybe not too far away, you may be charging your cell phone with a mushroom battery. Today's lithium-ion batteries are made with graphite. Graphite is expensive, and the chemicals used to make graphite damage the environment.

Imagine atoms moving back and forth, storing and releasing energy. These moving atoms make it possible for us to charge batteries, use them, and recharge them again.

To experiment with mushroom batteries, engineers make a nanoribbon by burning the skin from a mushroom cap several times at very high temperatures. These nanoribbons are porous, which means there's a lot of space for atoms to move back and forth — even more space than in graphite. Engineers hope that mushroom nanoribbons could help batteries last longer. They would also cost less and be better for the environment, too.

RECYCLED TREATS

An Austrian design firm has invented a way to turn plastic trash into human food. First, plastic is loaded into cup-like pods made from a seaweed-based gelatin. Next, fungi are added to the pods. After a few months, the fungi have eaten the plastic! Fill the edible fungi cup with fruit and yogurt and you have a healthy fungus treat that helped the environment.

BURIED WITH MUSHROOMS?

It may sound scary, but we all die at some point. Recently, people who care about the environment have been searching for better ways to bury the dead because ground burials and cremations release many toxins into the environment.

A scientist studying ways to use mycelium to break down toxins in the environment came up with a unique idea: a mushroom suit! Mushrooms and other microorganisms are woven into the suit. When someone dies, he or she is buried in the biodegradable suit. As the mushrooms grow, they decompose the body without damaging the environment. Mushrooms even break down toxins from medicines, tobacco, and other toxins in bodies. Later, plants can absorb the leftover nutrients. What do you think?

WHY NOT?

Look around. How much plastic do you see? Scientists and designers have come up with cool ways to make packaging and furniture from fungus instead of plastic. Some fungi-made items turn out like cork or rubber, while others are very hard.

To make containers, a mixture of mycelium and plant fibers is placed in a mold or pattern. As the fungus grows around the fibers, it fills the empty spaces. Next, the mycelium is dried in large kilns to stop it from growing.

A designer from the Netherlands created a 3D printer that can print mycelium to make furniture such as chairs and stools. He makes a paste with mycelium, water, and a plant waste such as straw. He prints a potato starch shell, and fills it in with the paste. As the fungus grows, it binds everything together. After it dries, the fungus furniture is strong enough to support the weight of a person!

Fungus-based items can be decomposed back into the environment, without releasing toxins. Eric Klarenbeek, designer of the fungus chair shown above, says, "Mushrooms, the emperors of our planet, can enable us to abandon our chain of waste."

43

DISEASE FIGHTERS

When scientists research new medicines, they often look at chemicals made by fungi, animals, plants, and bacteria. Medicines made from fungi have already saved millions of lives, and new fungi research may save millions more.

SHOTS FOR TREES?

About forty years ago, biologists in the Netherlands invented a vaccine to protect Dutch elm trees from a deadly fungus. When fungi spores are injected into their sap, the trees start working to protect themselves. The vaccine works well 99 percent of the time, but the trees need another shot every year.

RESEARCH MATTERS

Pesticides and herbicides may kill disease-causing fungi, but they can also pollute nearby soil, air, and water. After a while, the pesticides and herbicides may not work as well, and stronger chemicals are used, causing more pollution that can move through food webs.

Sometimes, one fungus can be used instead of pesticides or herbicides to kill disease-causing fungi. In the photo below, three types of biologists are working to make a fungicide: a microbiologist, a botanist, and an entomologist. These biologists study microbes, plants, and insects. In the photo to the right, a plant disease biologist grows a fungus for a fungicide by feeding it liquid food. Why does it matter what kind of food the fungus eats? Research shows the fungus makes toxins that can make people sick when the same fungus feeds on solid food.

FUNGI AT WORK

Thousands of years ago, ancient Egyptians placed moldy bread on cuts and wounds to fight infection.

In the late 1920s, Alexander Fleming noticed that bacteria were not growing near a mold in one of his Petri dishes. Years later, the first antibiotic, penicillin, was made in a factory. Since then, penicillin may have saved more than eighty million lives.

Decades later, Japanese scientist Akira Endo discovered a fungus chemical used to make a group of heart disease drugs called statins. Akira studied chemicals from more than two hundred types of fungi before finding one that worked. A few cancer drugs made from fungi are being tested now.

SAVING BEES

Recently, beekeepers have seen dangerous declines in the bee populations around the world. Colony collapse disorders (CCDs) cause about a 30 percent loss of beehives each year. Bees are important to humans because they pollinate about a third of plant crops. Scientists are trying to find out whether fungi can help immune systems in bees and whether fungi can control dangerous mites in hives.

NEW MEDICINE FROM ANCIENT MEDICINE?

High up on the Himalayan plains, a fungus attaches itself to ghost moth larvae burrowed in soil. The fungus feeds inside the larvae, killing and mummifying the moth from the inside. In the spring long, thin stalks appear and produce spores. This zombie fungus may become part of a drug for people with osteoarthritis, a painful type of arthritis.

These mushrooms have been a part of Asian medicine for hundreds of years. The mushrooms only grow in one place and cannot be farmed, making them hard to find and expensive. In England, scientists have been feeding pellets made from these mushrooms to rats and mice to find out if they can lower swelling and pain. Chemicals in these mushrooms seem to work differently than other arthritis medicines, but researchers are still trying to find out why.

45

TREATS

The idea of fungus as food may gross you out. Even if you don't like pizza mushrooms or blue cheese, though, you probably eat many foods made from fungus.

RISE, BABY, RISE!

Every living cell needs energy, including the yeast people use to make foods and drinks. When yeast make energy, they release carbon dioxide. This gas causes bread and donut dough to rise, filling it with air that makes the baked foods soft and light. Pizza dough is made with yeast, too. Yum.

SWEET TREATS

Many kinds of tart or sour candies use citric acid for flavor. Instead of getting citric acid from citrus fruits such as lemons and oranges, candy companies get fungi to make their citric acid. It's much faster and costs a lot less.

CHEESE!

Have you ever taken a bite of pizza or string cheese and been surprised by how far you can stretch mozzarella cheese? The cheese needs to be made with citric acid to be stretchy. Blue cheese (below) is made by adding a *Penicillium* fungus to the cheese as it's being made. It's moldy on purpose!

TEST IT OUT

IN ABOUT AN HOUR, YOU CAN MAKE TWO BATCHES OF MOZZARELLA CHEESE, ONE WITH CITRIC ACID AND ONE WITHOUT. HOW MUCH STRETCHIER IS THE CHEESE MADE WITH CITRIC ACID? CAN YOU THINK OF A WAY TO MEASURE THE DIFFERENCE?

Ask a grown-up to help you get the materials and cook on the stove. (Grown-ups are usually very helpful when they realize they will soon have homemade mozzarella cheese.)

WHAT YOU NEED FOR EACH BATCH

½ gallon whole milk

10 drops liquid rennet

Wooden kitchen spoon

½ teaspoon citric acid; *only for stretchy cheese!*

Large funnel or strainer

Cheese cloth or several layers of damp paper towels

Cooking thermometer

2 pans for double boiler

Salt to taste

Hot peppers, garlic powder, and/or herbs such as oregano or basil if you want extra flavor

WHAT TO DO

1. Pour the milk into the top pan of a double boiler. *If you are making a batch of stretchy cheese, stir in the citric acid now.* Fill the bottom pan halfway with water. Heat the milk on a stovetop to 90 degrees F (32° C).

2. Remove the milk mixture from the stove. Add the rennet drops and stir for two minutes. Season with a little salt and extra flavors if you like. Allow the mixture to thicken.

3. Strain the thickened mixture through your funnel with cheesecloth or damp paper towels over a cup or bowl. Liquid whey will drip out of the funnel, and cheese curds will be left!

WEATHER

You probably know that one of the important things about trees is that they take in carbon dioxide and release oxygen. But did you know that some underground fungi also take in a lot of carbon? Scientists are starting to look at how these fungi affect Earth's climate.

IMPACTING CLIMATE

When more carbon is in the atmosphere, the Earth heats up more. Soil, plants, and even the ocean are places where carbon is stored.

TREES & CARBON

Trees and other plants remove carbon dioxide from the atmosphere during photosynthesis. During this process, plants make sugar and release oxygen back into the atmosphere. When plants die or lose their needles or leaves, the carbon goes into the soil and stays there until the plant decomposes. Then, carbon from the dead plant releases back into the atmosphere.

CO_2

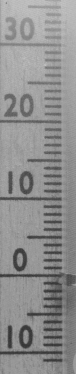

48

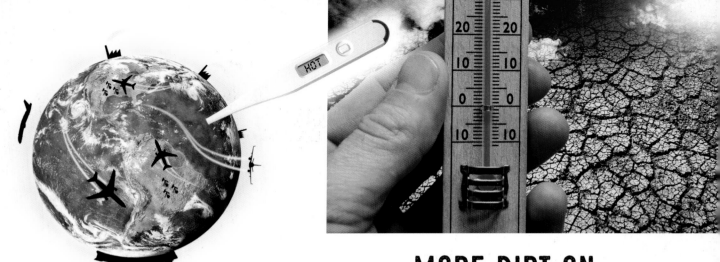

MORE DIRT ON MYCORRHIZAE

Underground fungi hold huge amounts of carbon, more than the soil and atmosphere together! Soils with mycorrhizae hold up to 70 percent more carbon than soils without mycorrhizae do. When scientists studied soil samples from all over the world, they found that soils without mycorrhizae have more carbon at the surface, while soils with mycorrhizae have more carbon at deeper levels.

SLOWER SPEEDS

The fungi living underground with plant roots can take lots of nitrogen from the soil. Less nitrogen in the soil means less nitrogen for soil microbes, which slows down plant decomposition. When plant decomposition slows down, less carbon goes back into the atmosphere.

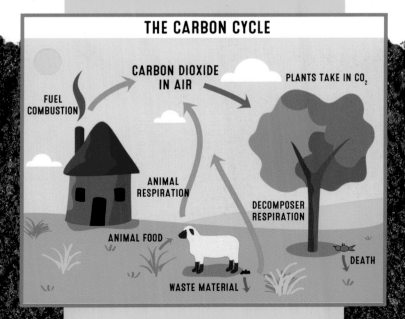

THE CARBON CYCLE

FUEL COMBUSTION

CARBON DIOXIDE IN AIR

PLANTS TAKE IN CO$_2$

ANIMAL RESPIRATION

DECOMPOSER RESPIRATION

ANIMAL FOOD

DEATH

WASTE MATERIAL

49

FUNGUS IN SPACE

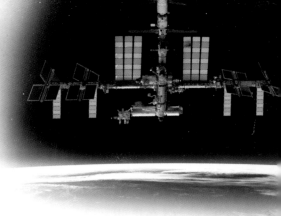

Does life really exist in outer space? Humans have been asking that question long before we left Earth. When we find other life forms in space, the big question is, did they hitchhike with humans or were they already there? Read more to find out!

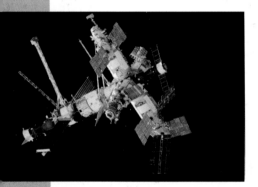

FUNGUS FINDERS

In 1988, a Russian cosmonaut looked out a window on the Mir space station. Instead of seeing Earth, he saw a mat of fungus covering the window. When cosmonauts looked more carefully at the ship, they saw it was covered with many types of fungi. They found fungi behind control panels, in the air conditioning unit, and on surfaces inside the station.

WHERE DID IT COME FROM?

Our homes are open systems. Air comes in and out of the house. Space stations are closed systems. Nothing from the outside is shared with the inside environment, which means the fungi didn't come from space. Instead, they came from living things inside the station. All people, even cosmonauts, carry fungi on their bodies.

The International Space Station (ISS), put into orbit in 1998, had fungus problems, too. Even though the spaceships were built in sterilized environments called "clean rooms," humans still brought fungi with them. The mold shown here is on a panel on the International Space Station in an area where astronauts hang up their clothes.

WHY SHOULD WE CARE?

The fungi that are found on the space stations are mostly harmless. Living with fungi is a natural thing here on Earth. The airtight environment of a space station is not a normal living condition, though. Spacecrafts are exposed to high levels of radiation. When fungi were found on the Mir space station, some scientists were worried that radiation could change the fungi, possibly making them more harmful to humans. It's also not good for metals and plastics on spaceships to be eaten by fungi!

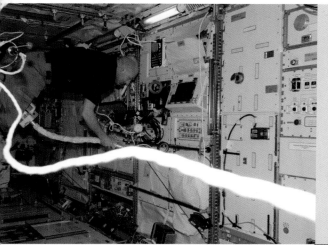

HOUSEKEEPING IN SPACE

To keep fungi away, astronauts clean space stations as part of their weekly chores, wiping down surfaces and vacuuming out air filters. Astronauts also monitor humidity levels to keep them between 65 and 70 percent because fungi like wet environments. Left: European Space Agency astronaut Andre Kuipers uses a vacuum cleaner on the International Space Station.

LAB ON BOARD!

Astronauts use a device to help them identify bacteria and fungi in space. A Lab-on-a-Chip Application Development-Portable Test System is a handheld lab. Astronauts sample microbes in the space station and get instant results. The lab app identifies the types of bacteria and fungi so astronauts know if the microbes are harmful. Astronauts will be able to use this tool to learn more about microbes they find in space. Right: Astronaut Sunita Williams, Expedition 15 flight engineer, works with the portable lab.

MISSIONS TO MARS

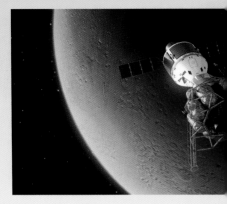

NASA is getting closer to sending astronauts to Mars. Because the trip will take three years, scientists must prepare for the long journey. Astronauts will need to grow some of their food.

SPACE GARDENING

Astronauts have grown plants on the International Space Station, and some of the plants developed fungi on them. Studying the conditions that cause fungi growth in space will help astronaut farmers on their journeys to Mars and back.

EXPERIMENTS IN SPACE

Scientists recently sent fungi into space. For the first experiment, they chose a fungus that grows in Antarctica. Researchers put a special container on a platform and attached it to the outside of the ISS. The fungus traveled outside the space station in harsh conditions for eighteen months. These conditions are very similar to the conditions on Mars. The scientists found the fungus survived in small corners and cracks of the container, where it was exposed to less radiation. Scientists may use this information to help them find life on Mars.

NO ALIEN SPECIES HERE

Since fungi may be able to live on Mars, humans need to be very careful not to bring Earth fungi there because it could damage the planet.

SPACE EFFECTS?

For the second experiment, scientists sent another fungus to space to test the effects of space conditions such as microgravity and high radiation on the fungus. Scientists wanted to know if space changes how fast the fungus grows and whether it will start making chemicals for new medicines. These medicines may be able to help astronauts with space-related health problems, or fight off disease-causing fungi and other disease.

WHAT DO YOU THINK, COLONEL FINCKE?

Astronaut Mike Fincke has spent more than three hundred days on space shuttles and the International Space Station. Colonel Fincke says, "Fungus, like anything else, can help us or hurt us. There is room for us to experiment and learn about fungus in space. Fungus may be helpful whenever astronauts prepare to go on long missions to Mars or the moon."

PLANT DISEASES

Fungi cause more than eight out of ten plant diseases. These diseases have some funny names that you may not have heard before, including rusts, smuts, powders, snow molds, blights, wilts, and root rots.

RUSTS, SMUTS & POWDERS

Rusts cause pimple-like shapes on leaves in orange, yellow, white, black, or brown. Smuts cause black powders on plants. Many white powders are mildews.

THINK IT THROUGH

Why do these diseases cause problems for plants? Check out the plants on these pages. When plants lose parts of their leaves, they have less space to make food through photosynthesis. When fungi damage roots, the plants get less water and fewer nutrients.

SEED FEEDERS

Fungi feed on seeds, too. In the photo to the left, the bright green area is a fungus working its way into a barley seed.

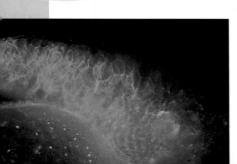

BLIGHT FIGHTS

Fungal diseases that kill leaves, flowers, stems, and roots are often called blights. Tomato blights cause problems every year for gardeners and farmers.

WILTING WILTS

On hot days, plants infected with a *Verticillium* fungus look sick. Their leaves and branches wilt, and they may lose their color. Sometimes they die. When one plant gets *Verticillium* wilt, nearby plants may get it, too, because the fungus can spread from one plant to another in the soil. The fungus can stay in the soil for years. More than four hundred types of plants, from trees to flowers to vegetables, can get *Verticillium* wilt.

CALL THE PLANT DOCTOR

Some fungal diseases can only be seen with microscopes. To find out whether trees have *Verticillium* wilt, plant biologists run a special test. They place small pieces of tree tissue in sugar water and wait a few days. If there's a fungus inside the plant, it will grow out through the plant and into the sugar water, where it can be seen with a microscope.

DISEASES

From the number of diseases shown in this book, you might think lots of fungi cause disease. Actually, only about three hundred kinds of fungi make people sick.

SNEEZING SPORES

Spores from mold, mildew, and other fungi can cause sneezing, runny noses, and other allergy problems. If you have these types of allergies, you should avoid damp and moldy places.

MORE SPORES

Because most fungi like moist habitats, you will usually find more spores in the air after rainy or foggy weather. Spore counts also go up at night, when air gets moister.

STAY DRY

Many fungal infections happen on the skin. They might seem gross, but don't be embarrassed. Most are easy to treat and easier to prevent. Ringworm is a fungal infection of the hair, skin, or nails that looks like red, circle-shaped sores. These circular rashes are not worms, and worms do not cause them. Some anti-fungal creams can treat ringworm infections.

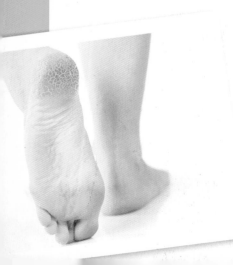

Athlete's foot is a fungal infection on feet and toenails that causes itching and burning. It's often worse in between toes. Athlete's foot is easy to prevent by washing and drying your feet every day, and wearing clean socks. The same fungus that causes athlete's foot causes jock itch, too. Because the fungus likes warm, moist areas, jock itch is often found on the thighs, buttocks, and groin area. It can be found on both males and females, and causes itching, burning, and chafing in the groin area. A doctor can suggest antifungal creams and sprays that will help.

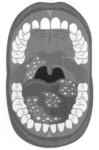

TRY NOT TO CRY

You've heard of baby rash, right? It's caused by the yeast *Candida*. These fungal infections can happen almost anywhere on the body, but candida likes warm, damp areas. Yeast infections cause rashes, pimple-like bumps, and itching or burning. One type of *Candida* grows in mouths and causes oral thrush.

DRY BUBBLE DISEASE

Fungi cause disease in more than just plants and animals. Fungi infect other fungi, too! One fungus infects the white button mushroom used on pizza with dry bubble disease. This disease can cause dead tissue that bubbles up, known as dry bubbles, or wet bubbles that leak fluid. Yuck.

WOOF!

Dogs can get yeast infections, too! Dogs get infected in moist areas such as their ears and paws, and infections can make them itch and even smell. This fungus is not the same one that infects humans. Luckily, dogs can be treated with creams, shampoos, and sprays. Your veterinarian may also prescribe medicine to help out.

TEENAGED TROUBLES

Another type of yeast rash is common on teenagers, and can be found all over the body. It is easy to prevent by washing yourself all over with dandruff shampoo about once a month.

LIVESTOCK DISEASE

Some fungal diseases in cows can make unborn calves sick. These diseases can affect other types of livestock, too.

57

SNACK ATTACK

The food in your kitchen is like an all-you-can-eat buffet for fungi. Remember, fungi eat the same sugars, proteins, and fats that you do. Kitchens can also make good fungi habitats because of heat and moisture from cooking.

HITCHHIKERS

Most fruits and vegetables come home from the grocery store or farmers' market with mold spores on them. The cold air in refrigerators can slow down mold growth.

DARK PLACES

Foods left in dark places such as in pizza boxes — or, ahem, under your bed — often mold faster.

SALT SHAKERS

Many foods that aren't kept in refrigerators are made with a lot of extra salt. The salt makes the food less moist, which makes it less appealing to fungi. Salt may also affect fungi cells. Don't believe it? Test it out!

TEST IT OUT

ALTHOUGH YOU CANNOT COUNT SINGLE MOLD SPORES ON BREAD SLICES WHEN YOU BEGIN THIS EXPERIMENT, YOU WILL BE ABLE TO SEE AND SMELL MOLD COLONIES AT THE END OF THE EXPERIMENT.

WHAT YOU NEED

5 slices of store-bought white bread

5 slices of homemade or preservative-free white bread

40 sealable sandwich bags

2 paper towels or napkins

Butter knife

Permanent marker

2 plastic or paper grocery bags or shoe boxes

WHAT TO DO

1. Place a slice of store-bought bread onto a paper towel or napkin and cut it into four even pieces. Place each piece inside a sandwich bag and seal it well. Repeat with the remaining four slices. Label each bag with a number from one through twenty. Throw away the paper towel or napkin.

2. Repeat step 1 with the homemade or preservative-free bread.

3. Place all of your store-bought bread in a bag or box and label it. Do the same thing with the homemade or preservative-free bread. Place the bread in a dark place where it will not be disturbed — dark closets and basements work well.

4. Check your bread samples every week for six weeks. If you are doing this experiment for a school project, make twelve data sheets with notebook paper or a computer. Label the top of each sheet with the type of bread and the week number, and list the numbers 1 through 20 so that each number gets its own line.

5. To record your data, use a measuring stick to carefully measure how much of each piece of bread is covered in mold. This number can be recorded as a percentage on your data sheet. Another way you can record data is to just record the presence or absence of mold in each bag. Use a + sign for presence and a − sign for absence. Be sure to list each data point on the corresponding line number on your data sheet.

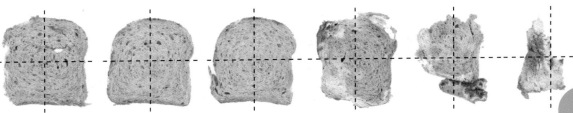

MOLD MESSES

Mold messes may gross us out, but they can usually be cleaned up with a little work. It doesn't mean you're dirty if there's mold in your house. Remember, fungus spores are everywhere, and if they land in the right spot, they will grow.

HOME, SWEET HOME

Every time we run bath or shower water, we make the bathroom a better habitat for mold. Some kitchens can attract mold, too — the moisture from cooking steam makes mold feel right at home.

CLOSET MOLD

Dark closets make good homes for mold, especially on shoes that may have become damp or wet outside. Items that we don't use much can get moldy, too.

60

OUTDOOR MOLD

Mold can grow on brick, wood, and other outdoor house surfaces. You will see more of it in damp places that do not get a lot of sun.

BYE-BYE, MOLD

A little scrubbing with vinegar or bleach can clean up mold messes. Don't be surprised when the mold comes back, though!

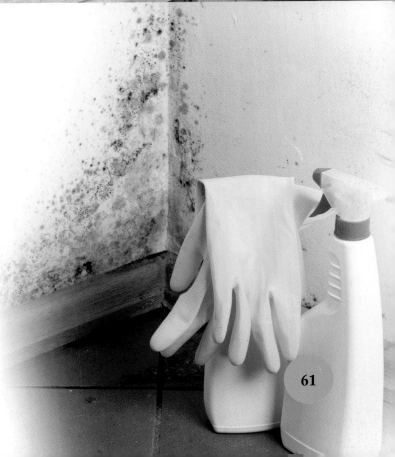

SCARY INFECTIONS

Some fungal infections can cause diseases with gross symptoms. Other fungi can cause problems that scare us when we think about them.

FROM BAD TO SCARY

The oral thrush and athlete's foot diseases you learned about earlier can go from bad to scary pretty quickly. In scary cases of oral thrush, infected patches on the tongue can ooze fluid. Bad cases of athlete's foot can cause bleeding as the fungus feeds through top layers of skin.

BARBER'S ITCH

Ringworm fungi can also infect beards and mustaches that cause itching and leave bald patches. Beard and mustache fungi can also cause flaking or blistered skin.

FUNKY FEET

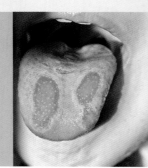

Feet have an average of fifty types of fungi on them. It's no wonder that toenails can get fungal infections, too. Toenail fungus can get really gross if untreated. Toenails may get thick, distorted, dark in color, and even separate from the nail bed.

PARASITES

Some fungi live as parasites in the intestines of humans and other animals. One group of fungal parasites infects people exposed to contaminated water. They reproduce quickly by fusing their cells to host cells, causing diarrhea, brain infections, and other problems.

62

VALLEY FEVER

Valley fever is caused by the fungus that lives in the soil in North America in parts of the west and southwest. The spores of the fungus move into the air when wind, plowing, construction, or even strong earthquakes disturb soil. When the spores are breathed in, they move to the lungs. Some people do not get sick from the spores. Others get mild cases of valley fever that go away on their own in a few weeks. These people may have coughs, fevers, headaches, rashes, and feel very tired. In a few people, valley fever lasts for months or even a lifetime.

BRAIN INFECTIONS?

When scientists studied the brains of people who had died with Alzheimer's disease, they found fungus in several parts of the brain and nearby blood vessels. Did the fungus cause Alzheimer's disease in these people? Or did the disease make it easier for the fungus to infect the brains? Scientists still have a lot to learn.

FLOODING MOLD

When hurricanes, melting snow, and heavy rains cause homes to flood, fungi can quickly take over. Some fungi feed on the sugars in drywall, while others feed on wood floors and carpeting.

ANIMAL SCARES

Over the last ten years, a fungus has killed more than six million bats in parts of North America. White-nose syndrome infects noses, ears, and wings while bats hibernate. White-nose syndrome spreads easily from one bat to another. Another fungus causes snake fungal disease in North American snakes. This soil fungus causes sores in their scales, and many snakes with snake fungal disease die. It may be the fungus that kills them. Or maybe the sores on their scales make them molt more often, which causes them to eat less and makes them more vulnerable to other diseases and predators.

FUNGAL DISEASES

Fungi cause big problems for more than just amphibians. Plants and aquatic animals are dying off, too.

VOLCANO FLOWERS

In the native forests of Hawaii, a fungus has killed thousands of ohia trees on several islands. Why does it matter if just one type of tree dies off in a forest? Ohia flowers, known as volcano flowers, feed nectar to many animals. Ohia trees collect water and add it to the watershed. Their leaves make shade for smaller trees. People can move the fungus from one island to another if they are not careful.

BYE-BYE, BANANAS?

At least three kinds of fungi are killing banana plants around the world. Scientists are working hard to solve this problem.

CORAL DISEASES

As corals become more stressed from pollution and warmer waters, biologists have found more corals with diseases caused by fungi and other microbes. About 25 percent of the world's marine animals live in coral ecosystems so healthy corals are important.

CHESTNUT BLIGHT

In the early 1900s, a fungal disease killed more than three and a half *billion* chestnut trees in North American forests. When these trees died, habitats and food for many animals were also lost. Young chestnut trees can still be found in these forests, but they die from the fungus blight in just a few years.

Today, biologists are working with chestnut trees from China and Japan to help North American chestnuts. Because the Asian trees have some immunity to the fungus, biologists may be able to cross the species so that the North American trees will get genes for immunity. Other biologists are researching a virus that protects some chestnut trees from the disease-causing fungus.

FUNGUS FOOD

Fungi also feed on many fish eggs, and some fish spend a lot of time cleaning their eggs so fungi can't grow on them. Right: fungus feeding on catfish eggs.

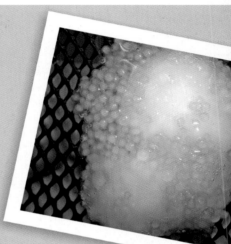

FISH FUNGI

Fungi cause many types of fish disease. This flatfish was infected with a fungus parasite.

GROUND NESTS

To a fungus, a ground nest full of eggs makes a fine meal. Soil fungi can cause disease or death in alligator, crocodile, and turtle eggs. How do they get inside the eggs? They dissolve the shells as they eat their way through them.

EXTINCTION

More amphibians are endangered than any other kind of vertebrate animal, and fungus is one reason why. At least a hundred amphibians have gone extinct in the last thirty years from fungal infections. Many others are endangered or critically endangered.

BRING YOUR PAINTBRUSH

When a fungus feeds on an amphibian's skin, it makes small scrapes that bacteria can infect. Too much fungus on an amphibian's skin can also keep it from getting enough oxygen. In some places, people try to help frogs by painting fungus-killing medicine onto frog skin.

FAVORITE FROGS

People often use brightly colored poison dart frogs as examples of rain forest animals and their ecosystems. Do you think people will want to learn more about fungus when they learn it may be hurting frogs?

FIRE SALAMANDERS

In the Netherlands, a fungus has killed most of the wild fire salamanders. The number of fire salamanders in many other places is going down.

GUILTY GEESE?

Scientists in Belgium found frog-killing fungus on the webbed feet of two different types of geese. As the geese fly from pond to pond, they may be bringing the fungus with them.

GUILTY PEOPLE?

Biologists believe the chytrid (ki trid) fungus that's killing amphibians around the world may have come from South Africa more than fifty years ago. People may have moved the fungus to other places when they imported frogs and salamanders for pets and medicines.

GOOD NEWS, BAD NEWS

Chytrid fungi cannot live everywhere. They need cool, moist places, and so do their spores. Unfortunately, the moist layer of mucus that helps many amphibians breathe through their skin makes a good habitat for fungus. Most amphibians also begin their lives in water, where the chytrid fungus can infect tadpoles.

ZOMBIE & MUMMY FUNGI

Can a fungus really be a zombie or a mummy? No, but can these parasites turn the animals they live inside into zombies? Yes, they can. These zombie animals don't behave like human zombies or mummies in books and movies, but they do some pretty wild things.

ZOMBIE ANTS

Zombie ant fungi live as parasites, using both birds and ants to complete their life cycles. Birds become infected with zombie fungi when they eat fake berries filled with zombie ant fungi. The birds release fungi spores with their feces. When ants feed on bird poop, they infect themselves with zombie ant fungi.

Zombie fungi cause growths on ant heads, which look like berries to the birds flying above. Ants infected with zombie ant fungi do not hide from predators. Instead, they stay out in the open, where birds are more likely to find them. Why? The fungus infects their nervous system, which changes their behavior.

ZOMBIE STICKS

A fungus parasitized this stick insect in Madagascar. First, spores infected its nervous system. Later, the fungus fed on the dead insect and released more spores.

MUMMY BEES

Biologists have found more than sixty causes of colony collapse disorders in bees. A fungus that infects larvae while they're pupating is one cause. Infected larvae are called mummies because they are long and white.

MORE ZOMBIES

A zombie fungus infected these animals in a rain forest in Ecuador. Clockwise from top left: a spider, a moth, a fly, and a beetle

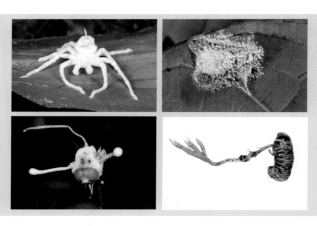

ZOMBIE FROGS

Fungus infections can make some frogs spend more time on land. The frogs also move less and move more slowly, making it easier for hungry predators to catch them. Some infected frogs jump or swim in circles. Others cannot turn themselves right-side up if they fall over.

New research shows that one type of fungus changes the mating calls of some male frogs. The males called longer and sang their songs faster, making them sound better to females, which could spread more fungi. This research was done with Japanese tree frogs. Biologists will repeat the research with larger numbers of frogs and different types of frogs.

FREAKING OUT OVER FUNGI

For all the wonderful ways fungi make plant lives better, they can also cause some serious problems.

LOST FOOD

When fungi damage or kill just five types of crops, they take away food from six hundred million people around the world. These five crops are soybeans, potatoes, corn, wheat, and rice. More than four billion people on Earth rely on one or more of these crops to keep them from starving. Fungi damage to crops costs farmers more than $60 billion every year.

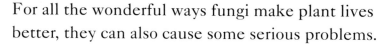

LEAVE THE FUNGI AT HOME!

As humans move more and more things around the world, we move more and more disease-causing fungi with us. Some places in the world won't let people bring fresh fruits, vegetables, and plants across borders.

TOO MUCH CO$_2$

Every tree, bush, or shrub that dies from a fungal disease is one less plant that can pull extra CO_2 from the air. Biologists say that the trees killed or damaged by fungi could have absorbed between 230 and 589 megatons of CO_2. How does this extra CO_2 affect temperatures on Earth?

BLAME A FUNGUS?

Most people don't think about fungus very often, but it's caused some pretty big problems for humans. Many times, though, humans are part of the problem.

SPELL-CASTING MOLDS?

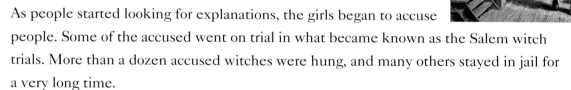

In the winter of 1692 in a village in Salem, Massachusetts, young girls began having strange spasms and fits. When doctors couldn't find a cause, their behavior was blamed on witchcraft.

As people started looking for explanations, the girls began to accuse people. Some of the accused went on trial in what became known as the Salem witch trials. More than a dozen accused witches were hung, and many others stayed in jail for a very long time.

One theory behind the spasms and fits is tied to fungus. A scientist who studies behavior researched the girls' strange fits and spasms. She traced the cause to a fungus.

Ergot is a type of fungus that grows on grain. This fungus is linked to a drug that causes strange behavior in people. Ergot only grows in warm, wet conditions, just like the summer of 1691.

The theory is that ergot-infected grain was stored and later made into bread. The girls who had spasms and fits lived on family farms where this grain was grown. The next summer was drier and no ergot grew on the grains. Before the Salem witch trials ended, more than 150 people had been accused of witchcraft.

TRAVELING MOLD

In the 1870s, a grape mold from the US almost wiped out the entire French wine industry. How did a fungus from the US end up in France? French winemakers wanted to grow grapes that could fight off aphids that were feeding on roots. Their plan was to cross grape plants from the US with plants from France to make a super plant that could resist aphids. Unfortunately, mold traveled to France on the US grape plants. The water mold spread quickly through France's vineyards, and thousands of acres had to be destroyed.

STARVING MOLDS

In the mid-1800s, a fungus wiped out potato crops in northern Europe and Ireland. The fungus feeds on leaf tissue, which means the plants cannot make as much food because they have less leaf surface for photosynthesis. When plants don't have enough food, they cannot support the potatoes growing underground from their roots.

At the time in Ireland, many people lived solely on potatoes. Because of the fungus, more than a million Irish people died from disease and starvation. Another two million Irish people left the country to find other homes. Where did this fungus come from? Biologists believe it traveled on potato plants stored on ships moving from South America, the native home of potatoes, to Europe.

Why are biologists so sure a fungus caused the Great Potato Famine? They aren't just guessing. Instead, they looked at the DNA from museum samples of potato plants in the mid-1800s. By looking at DNA base pairs, they knew it was a fungus and could even tell which species it was. This same fungus still causes plant damage to crops around the world.

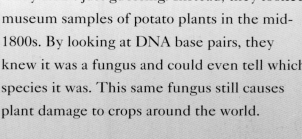

HUMONGOUS FUNGUS

The largest living thing on Earth isn't a blue whale or even a redwood tree. It's a fungus with a fun name: humongous fungus. People who live nearby celebrate their fungus with a festival every August. How do you celebrate a fungus? With a parade, fireworks, and the world's largest mushroom pizza, of course.

HOW GINORMOUS IS IT?

Humongous fungus lives mostly underground in North America in the Blue Mountains of Oregon. It covers about 3.4 miles (8.4 km^2). Biologists think humongous fungus is about two thousand years old, but some say it could be up to eight thousand years old. That's one old fungus! Other huge fungi have been found in North America in Washington and Michigan, and in Europe. The best way to see humongous fungus is to look for its honey mushrooms in the fall at the bases of trees. They are edible, but don't taste like honey.

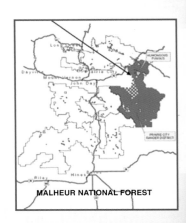

MALHEUR NATIONAL FOREST

A KILLER FUNGUS

Humongous fungus is a parasite, and its long, black, thickened hyphae spread over tree roots. Eventually, the trees cannot get nutrients and begin to die. To find out if this huge underground mass was one big organism or many smaller ones, biologists used DNA to test the hyphae in many places, including the very edges. Scientists used the hyphae locations to learn how fast the hyphae grow and to estimate humongous fungus's age. The hyphae grow faster than you do: up to three feet (0.9 m) a year!

DEADLY FUNGI

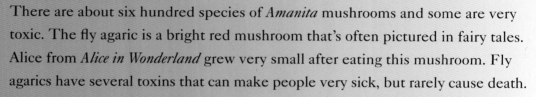

Go walking through the woods and you're likely to see many types of mushrooms. Some of them are edible, but others can make people very sick or even cause death.

TOXIC TALES

There are about six hundred species of *Amanita* mushrooms and some are very toxic. The fly agaric is a bright red mushroom that's often pictured in fairy tales. Alice from *Alice in Wonderland* grew very small after eating this mushroom. Fly agarics have several toxins that can make people very sick, but rarely cause death.

The destroying angel is another *Amanita* mushroom. Named for its stark white color and deadly toxins, the destroying angel is one of the most poisonous mushrooms in North America and Europe.

THE FAKER

Morel mushrooms are edible and considered a delicacy, but there's an imposter out there! The false morel looks a lot like true morels. If people eat a false morel by mistake, the results can be dangerous. Depending on the toxin level, false morels can cause flu-like symptoms, serious illness, or even death.

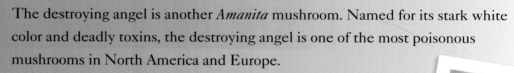

AUTUMN SKULLCAP

The autumn skullcap is found from the Arctic to Australia. Its brown to yellowish mushrooms are often confused with several small, brown, nontoxic mushrooms. If eaten, it can cause liver damage and death.

MUSHROOM SAFETY

If you want to learn more about hunting wild mushrooms, it's important to learn how to identify them from a good mushroom identification book and always hunt with an expert. Dogs can get very ill from toxic mushrooms, just like people, so watch them carefully.

BACTERIA
Single-celled organisms that do not have organelles

CAMOUFLAGE
To blend in with the environment

CARBOHYDRATE (ALSO CALLED SUGAR)
A type of organic molecule made from carbon, oxygen, and hydrogen. Simple carbohydrates give animals energy; complex carbohydrates are structures such as cell walls in fungi and plants, and exoskeletons in arthropods.

CELL
The smallest unit of life. Cells with membrane-bound organelles are eukaryotes; cells without membrane-bound organelles are prokaryotes.

CHITIN
A complex carbohydrate found in the cell walls of fungi and the exoskeletons of arthropods

DECOMPOSER
An organism that feeds on and breaks down dead or decaying plants or animals and returns nutrients to the ecosystem. Bacteria and fungi are common decomposers.

DNA (DEOXYRIBONUCLEIC ACID)
The chemical makeup of an organism's genes

ECOSYSTEM
The living and nonliving parts of an environment that function together as a group

ENZYME
A type of protein that speeds up reaction rates

FOOD WEB
The interactions and energy flow between many food chains

HABITAT
The home for an organism or a group of organisms

HYPHA/HYPHAE (SINGULAR/PLURAL)
Branching filaments that form colonies called mycelia

LICHEN
A two- or three-way symbiosis between a fungus, an alga, and/or a cyanobacterium

LIPID
A type of organic molecule made from carbon, oxygen, and hydrogen that provides long-term energy to animals

MUTUALISM
A type of symbiosis that is beneficial to the organisms involved

MYCELIUM/MYCELIA (SINGULAR/PLURAL)
A colony of hyphae; also known as the vegetative part of a fungus

PARASITE
An organism that lives in or on another organism (host) and benefits by taking nutrients from the host

PREDATOR

An organism that preys on other organisms

PREY

An animal being hunted or eaten by another animal

PROTEIN

A large molecule made from amino acids; some proteins are enzymes.

SOIL

The solids, liquids, and gases that occur on the surface of land; includes both living organisms and nonliving materials

SPORE

Small, seed-like reproduction units in fungi

SYMBIOSIS

Two or more organisms living closely together and interacting

TOXIN

A substance that can harm a living organism

YEAST

A type of single-celled fungi

WILD NAMES, WILD STORIES

DOG NOSE FUNGUS (above left) earned its name because it looks like a cat's wet nose. *A cat's nose?* Ah, you're right. It was named after a dog's nose. (Just checking to see if you're reading.) Spores shoot out of the small, wet areas.

ICE HAIR (above right) was first noted about a hundred years ago. This beautiful, strange ice looks like hair coming off someone's head. It can last for a few days or just a few hours. Ice hair forms on winter nights in latitudes between 45°N and 55°N, when temperatures hover right below freezing. Biologists who study this ice formation have found that one kind of fungus is always present in rotting wood when ice hairs form.

WITCHES BUTTER (opposite page, far left) is a type of jelly fungus that earned its name because of a legend about witches. According to the legend, if you find a witches butter fungus near your home, someone has cast a spell on you.

DEVIL'S TOOTH FUNGUS (opposite page, far right), also known as bleeding tooth fungus, often lives under evergreen trees. The red liquid that looks like blood is really the protein that gives many mushrooms their red color.

77

Information from the following individuals, places, and organizations contributed greatly to this book:

Michael Achatz, Cat Adams, Andrea Aerts, Albert Einstein College of Medicine, Ruth Alonso, Philip Alsen, American Physical Society's Division of Fluid Dynamics, Deuknam An, Stacey Anderson, Meinrat Andreae, Sandra L. Anganostakis, A. Elizabeth Arnold, Asthma and Allergy Foundation of America (AAFA), Colin Averill, Frank Aylward, Rajesh Bajpai, David Baker, Malina A. Bakowski, Keir M. Balla, Eben Bayer, S. W. Behie, Trudy E. Bell, I. Berlanger, David M. Beyer, M. J. Bidochka, Antonio Biraghi, Jason Bittel, Lynne Boddy, Paola Bonfante, C. S. Boon, Boundless, Emily Bourke, Cheryl J. Briggs, John S. Brownstein, Ruth A. Bryan, Bugwood, Brennan Campbell, Linda Caporael, Jean Carlier, Ada Carr, Luis Carrasco, Arturo Casadevall, Anne Casselman, Center for Disease Control and Prevention, Charles Q. Choi, Jon Cohen, Gareth Cook, Clive Cookson, Daniel A. Cossins, James Costa, Charles F. Crane, Cameron Currie, Ekaterina Dadachova, Diana Davis, Tristan V. de Jong, Rosa de la Torre, Cornelia H. De Moor, Jean-Pierre de Vera, Ineke de Vries, Gaby Deckmyn, David Derrer, Braham Dhillon, Caucasella Diaz-Trujillo, Robert Dietrich, Discover Tasmania, Pradeep K. Divakar, Jim Dixon, Mark Double, Emilie Dressaire, Ecovative, A. Ekbald, Kelly Elkins, Everglades Research & Education Center/University of Florida, Andrew D. Farmer, Eric Feinberg, Claudia Fortes Fereira, Becky Ferreira, Michael Finke, Michael Finkel, Adrien Finzi, Joshua Fisher, Mark Fisher, Matthew Fisher, Alastair Fitter, Nic Fleming, Althea Flemming, Nick Flemming, Greg Flip, James A. Foley, Jennifer Frazer, Ian Frazier, Suzana Garcia, Andrea Genre, Elizabeth Goldbaum, Sam Ohu Gon III, Bob Grant, Neal Grantham, T. Grebec, Veronique Greenwood, Rupal Christine Gupta, Sarah J. Gurr, Mauricio Guzman, Richard Hammond, Maribeth Hassett, Robert Hauff, David Hawksworth, Daniel A. Henk, J. E. Henny, Joan Henson, David Hibbett, Sarah Higginbotham, Angela Hodge, Anne-Marie Hodge, Kathie Hodge, Diana Hofmann, Gregory A. Hoover, Gerda Horneck, Elizabeth Howell, Xianchun Huang, Bruce Hungate, E. Iglich, Elaine R. Ingham, Integrated Taxonomic Information System, Rafael E. Arango Isaza, Liliana Iturrado, Ferris Jabr, David Johnson, Elizabeth Keller, Gert H. J. Kema, Kew Royal Botanic Gardens, Eric Klarenbeek, A. Komarov, H. Kraigher, Sarah Kramer, Jacquelyn J. Kremser, C. Mike Kuo, Lawrence Berkeley National Laboratory, Chris Reid, Roger G. Linington, Livin Studio, Jeffrey Lorch, Robert J. Luallen, H. H. Lyon, Bill MacDonald, Fiona Macrae, Lawrence C. Madoff, Douglas Main, Barbara Maranzani, L. M. Marquez, Christian Matzler, Max Planck Institute for Chemistry, Mayo Clinic, Audrey Mcavoy, Gavin McIntyre, Kate Melville, A. Meyer, Miami University, Microbiology Society, Tiffany Moadel, Nicholas Money, Maurizio Montalti, Ceasar Terrer Moreno, Kathryn Morris, Nicholas Mott, Mount St. Joseph University, Danielle Muoio, Toshiyuki Nakagaki, National Aeronautics and Space Administration (NASA), National Institutes of Health, National Park Service/United States Department of the Interior, Natural Resources Conservation Service, Nature Conservancy of Hawaii, Joshua D. Nosanchuk, Natalia Novikova, Mandy Oaklander, Chloe Olewitz, Michelle O'Malley, Silvano Onofri, Mark Ott, Douglas Page, Catherine Parks, Vince Patton, Penn State College of Agricultural Sciences, Pennsylvania State Extension Agency, Duane L. Pierson, Diana Pisa, Christopher Pohlker, Michael Polsen, Ulrich Poschl, Susan Post, M. L. Powelson, Prairie Research Institute/Illinois Natural History Survey, Lisa Pratt, Gisela Preuss, Alberto Rabano, Elke Rabbow, Richard Raid, Regina Redman, Jae Rhim Lee, Chris Rhodes, Izaskun Rodal, Russell Rodriguez, Monsi Roman, Adriana Romero, Marcus Roper, Ken Russel, Michael Ryan, Anna Salleh, Giuliano Scalzi, Craig Schmitt, Louie Schwartzberg, Andrew D. Schweitzer, Science Daily, Laura Selbmann, Judy Seltzer, Terry Shaw, Steve Sheppard, Vertika Shukla, Suzanne Simard, W. A. Sinclair, Myron Smith, Smithsonian Museum of Natural History, M. M. Smits, Elizabeth Snouffer, Carmenza Spadafora, Paul J. Stamets, Andrew Steele, Rich Stout, Scott Strobel, Michael Tatum, Alejandro Tauber, C. L. Taylor, Madeleine Thomas, Richard Thorington, Silvana Tridico, Emily R. Troemel, Nicola Twilley, Katharina Unger, United States Department of Agriculture (USDA), United States Geographical Survey, University of California, Riverside, University of Texas at Austin, Dalip Kumar Upreti, Utrecht University, Kasthuri J. Venkateswaran, Stephen J. Vesper, Tom Volk, Bruce Waldman, Bryan Walsh, Clay Wang, Washington Department of Fish and Wildlife, Patricia Wiltshire, Weng Ruh Wong, Wing Wong, Han Wosten, Paul J. Wuest, Yale University Department of Molecular Biophysics and Biochemistry, Bob Yirka, P. M. Zelisko, Ren Sen Zeng, and Laura Zucconi

The authors extend their gratitude to the following photographers and photographic sources for their creative contributions:

3Dsculptor, 5 Second Studio, Adrian_am13, Africa Studio, Natalia Aggiato, Potapov Alexander, Alexsvirid, Alima007, Alpha Wolf/Wikimedia Commons, Alter-ego, Tommy Alven, Andscha, Anekoho, Jody Ann, Annettt, Anteromite, AppStock, Egorov Artem, Arttonick, AsherStock, Asyrafazizan, Stephen Ausmus/USDA, Aydngvn, Bakusova, Barry Barnes, Beornbjorn, Bikeriderlondon, Birdiegal, Barry Blackburn, Blan-k, Blue Ring Media, Bob.leccinum.Robert Kozak, Artur Bogacki, Ryan M. Bolton, Gerardo Borbolla, B. Brown, Axel Bueckert, Binh Thanh Bui, Canbedone, David Cappaert/Bugwood.org, Carroteater, Cheryl Casey/Shutterstock.com, Catchlight Lens, Cegli, Chaikom, Tawatchai Chaimongkon, Chalermsak, Igor Chernomorchenko, Robert Cicchetti, Cobalt88, Graham Corney, Cornel Constantin, Rachanon Cumnonchai, Comaniciu Dan, Roberto David, Francesco de Marco, Designua, DnD-Production.com, Miriam Doerr, Dohduhdah/Wikimedia Commons, Dream Master, EarthArts Photography, Dudakova Elena, Pixel Embargo, Dirk Ercken, Everett Historical, Exopixel, Dari Extension, Even Ezer, Geza Farkas, Melinda Fawver, Feel Photo Art, Frank Fiedler, Fivespots, Flydragonfly, Fotokostic, Martin Fowler, Martin Frommherz, Sanit Fuangnakhon, Rainer Fuhrmann, Filip Fuxa, J. Gade, Gam1983, Markus Gann, Geertweggen, Leszek Glasner, Bildagentur Zoonar GmbH, GraphicsRF, Peggy Greb/USDA, Grebcha, Fer Gregory, Richard Griffin, Tom Grundy, Guentermanaus, Gumbao, Gyn9037, Happy Stock Photo, Hddigital, Damian Herde, HHelene, Rob Hille, Hans Hillewaert/Creative Commons, Margrit Hirsch, Honglouwawa, Gertjan Hooijer, Nataliya Hora, Iadams, Indy Edge, Ioskutnikov, Irin-k, Tischenko Irina, IrinaK, Isak55, Eric Isselee, Iunewind, Dale Lorna Jacobsen, Jeabphoto-13, Jet Propulsion Laboratory.gov, Yongkiet Jitwattanatam, Jps, Korkiat Jumpa, Michael Jung, Kabukinut, Kaleidoscopik Photography, Sergey Kamshylin, Steven Katovich/USDA Forest Service/Bugwood.org, Sebastian Kaulitzki, Kevin, Kichigin, Kiri11, Erik Klarenbeek, Klerik78, Kletr, Graeme Knox, Nilce Naomi Kobori/USDA, Aleksandr Kovalev, Anton Kozyrev, Krasowit, Wolfgang Kruck, Ksenvitaln, Nikolay Kurzenko, Andrey Kuzmin, Kzww, Henrik Larsson, Karin Hildebrand Lau, Alexandra Lelbix, Lesa, Wang LiQiang, Livinstudio, Elisa Locci, Lorcel, Madlen, Magnetix, Markus Mainka, Dariusz Majgier, Darius Malinowski/USDA, Joyce Mar, Ivan Marjanovic, Brian Maudsley, Steve McWilliam, Mega Pixel, Melis, Meryll, Maurizio Milanesio, Mildenmi, Monning27, Gavin Morrison, Mr. High Sky, Mr.Kie, Maks Narodenko, NASA, NinaM, Nofilm2011, Norikazu, Joseph O'Brien/USDA Forest Service/Bugwood. org, OrelImages, Orla, Paul Paladin, Pandapaw, Paul Reeves Photography, Paulaphoto, Pavalena, Evgenii Pavlov, Petch One, Bardocz Peter, Igor Petrushenko, Jeff Pettis/USDA, Photo_master 2000/Shutterstock. com, Photographyfirm, Arnon Phutthajak, Picsfive, PKZ, Plasid, Pogonici, Prajit48, Ondrej Prosicky, Randimal, Valentina Razumovai, Morley Read, Ian Redding, Riopatuca, Kristo Robert, Alan Rockefeller/Wikimedia Commons, Panupan Rodpradit, Olha Rohulya, Manfred Ruckszio, Damian Ryszawy, Nancy S., Oliver S., Vadim Sadovski, Sergio Schnitzler, Nailia Schwarz, Sciencepics, Seashell World, Richard Seeley, Vova Shevchuk, ShutterPNPhotography/Shutterstock.com, Angel Simon, Ron Skadsen/USDA, Jarek Tuszy Ski/Wikimedia Commons, Christopher Slesarchik, Danny Smythe, Chatchai Somwat, Sonsam, Spiral Media, Sramey/Wikimedia Commons, Sruilk, Maria Starovoytova, Olya Steckel, Aleksey Stemmer, Stockthrone.com, Stockvision, Dave Straus/USDA, Studio 37, Studio Elepaio, Julia Sudnitskaya, Sue Burton PhotographyLtd, Sutham, Svitlana-ua, Taborsky, Chay Talanon, Sara Tarr, Dan Tautan, ThamKC, Decha Thapanya, Thatmacroguy, Shunfa The, Tiger Images, Timquo, TitoOnz, toeytoey, Tugolukof, TUM2282, Usanee, Julie Vader, Sujin Vaipia, Vectortone, Violetkaipa, Vipman, Vladvm, Vnlit, Robert Voight, Ryan von Linden/New York Department of Environmental Conservation, Julian W., Scott Walmsley, Tadeusz Wejkszo, Wolkenengel565, Wolna, Vladimir Wrangel, Sara Wright/USDA, Xpixel, Yellowrail, Jeff Zehnder, Yuangeng Zhang, Zhuda, and Zcw